Future Fashion

All real!
Though delivery
may be delayed
while scientists
turn new
discoveries into
actual clothes.

By Darlene Ivy
Art By Rupert van Wyk

Library For All Ltd.

Future Fashion

First published 2019

Published by Library For All Ltd
Email: info@libraryforall.org
URL: libraryforall.org

Originally published as Future Fashion by Darlene Ivy & Rupert van Wyk, 2019 © by Cricket Media,Inc. Reproduced with permission.

This book was made possible by the generous support of the June Canavan Foundation.

Original illustrations by Rupert van Wyk

Future Fashion
Ivy, Darlene
ISBN: 978-1-922374-96-7
SKU01061

Future Fashion

NEW Self-Repairing Suit

Are you sick of holes in your clothes? This new fabric repairs itself! If this cloth gets a hole, just rub the spot briskly. Heat from the rubbing will coax the fibres to link up again, sealing the hole. Hole? What hole?

Kevlar To The Rescue

A classic! Since it was invented in 1965, Kevlar and its cousin Nomex have been keeping firefighters and rescue workers safe. The special formula makes long, stretchy threads that don't burn and are hard to cut. Many layers make cloth that can stop a bullet.

NEW Spider Threads

Spider silk makes super strong cloth, if you can get enough of it. But spiders are tricky to farm. So scientists are using goats instead. They give goats a spider gene that makes a silk protein in their milk. Silk bits in the milk can then be spun into thread.

All Season Wear

Air-conditioned Shirt

Tired of being too hot or too cold? This new shirt will keep you feeling just right. When you're hot, the threads stretch a bit so the weave gets looser, like opening tiny windows to let heat out. When you're cold, the fibres tighten up to hold warmth in.

6

NEW Reversible Furnace

This coat can keep you warm or cool! Just flip it inside out. The cloth has layers coated with carbon and copper. On cold days, face the copper layer out. That reflects heat in, so you stay warm. When spring comes, turn the jacket inside out. Now the copper pulls heat from your body to keep you cool as a cucumber.

Clean Collection

NEW Self-Cleaning Shirt!

Never do laundry again with super dirt-shedding clothes! The fabric is inspired by lotus leaves. The threads are covered in very tiny spikes. Drops of water sit on top of the spikes and roll off, taking dirt with them. Just shake and it's clean!

Sun-No-Spot

To clean this shirt, just stand in the sun! A special outer layer soaks up UV light from the sun. This heats it up enough to zap stains. You stay cool, but stains fade away! Some stains vanish in minutes—tough ones might take a day.

New fabrics woven with thin metal wires inside can turn ordinary cloth into a touch screen or power source. The possibilities are endless!

New Styles for Spring!

Charging Shirt

Solar panels can make electricity—and so can this shirt. Ordinary cotton or wool is treated with a coating that converts light energy into electricity. Wires send the charge to a port or pocket.

NEW Wiggle Energy

This cloth gets a charge from running around. As you move, the fabric stretches and squishes. Thin wires in the fabric turn the motion into electrical energy. That flows to a plug to charge a device, or light up the buttons.

Touch Sleeve

The sleeve of this jacket is also a touch-screen! A computer the size of a button can read taps on a grid of thin wires in the cloth. Tap your sleeve to answer your phone, listen to a song, or move in a video game.

Chameleon Cloth

Tired of the same old look? How about clothes that change colour? This fabric is made with dyes that change colour when they get warm. A small battery heats up thin metal threads in the cloth, to change colours or make patterns.

NEW All Aglow

Thin electric wires and tiny batteries sewn into a dress or suit can power LED lights for a truly brilliant party look!

NEW Airbag Suit

Mountain climbers and bike racers love this special suit. The outside is wired up with motion sensors. When they detect a collision or fall, an airbag collar pops up. The whole suit puffs up with air, turning into a wearable pillow to cushion a fall.

Spider Sense

Feel your way around any room, even in the dark! This special jacket vibrates on the side that's approaching a wall, person, or other obstacle. If your right hand is near the door, your right sleeve buzzes. The jacket senses its surroundings with ultrasound, just like a bat.

NEW Training Suit

This shirt can help improve your game. As you run or play, sewn-on sensors track exactly how you move. An app uses the data to give feedback in real time. Straighten that leg! Take longer strides! Doctors can also use sensor suits to keep an eye on patients without hooking them up to bulky machines.

Power Assist

These pants do more than look sharp—they help the wearer stand or walk! The fabric has panels that stiffen when they feel electricity. Motion sensors can tell if you're trying to stand, or walk. Then a small computer activates the helping panels in the knees, or legs, or back—wherever a little lift is needed.

You can use these questions to talk about this book with your family, friends and teachers.

What did you learn from this book?

Describe this book in one word. Funny? Scary? Colourful? Interesting?

How did this book make you feel when you finished reading it?

What was your favourite part of this book?

download our reader app
getlibraryforall.org

About the contributors

Library For All works with authors and illustrators from around the world to develop diverse, relevant, high quality stories for young readers. Visit libraryforall.org for the latest news on writers' workshop events, submission guidelines and other creative opportunities.

Did you enjoy this book?

We have hundreds more expertly curated original stories to choose from.

We work in partnership with authors, educators, cultural advisors, governments and NGOs to bring the joy of reading to children everywhere.

Did you know?

We create global impact in these fields by embracing the United Nations Sustainable Development Goals.

Here are some other books you might like:

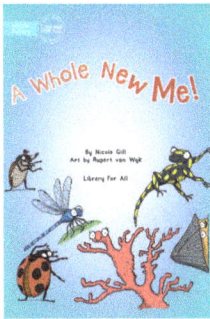

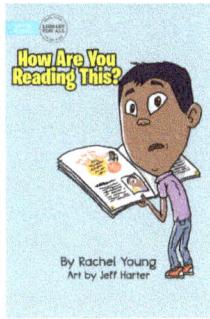

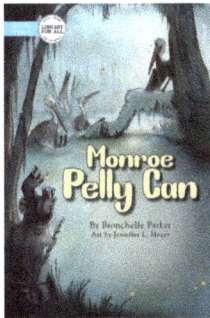

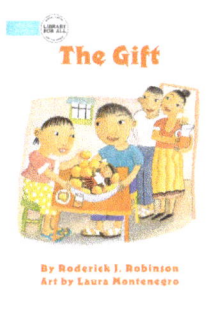

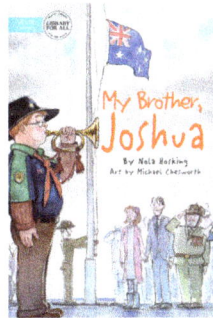

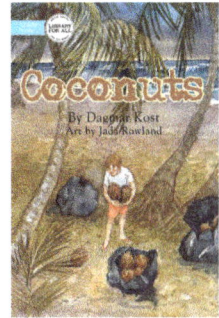

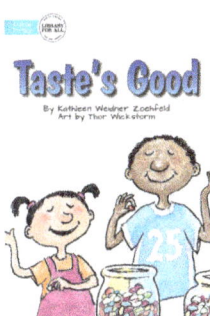

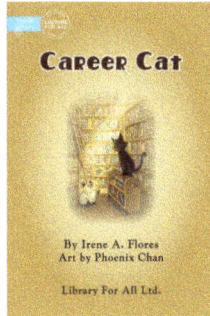

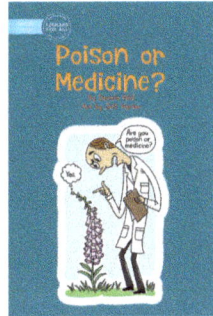

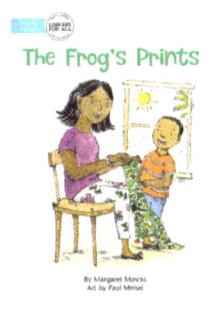

A Whole New Me!
By Nicola Gill
Art by Rupert van Wyk
Library For All

How Are You Reading This?
By Rachel Young
Art by Jeff Harter

MY EYE PATCH MADE ME AN AUTHOR
Jacob's Eye Patch
By Beth Koblinez Shaw And Jacob Shaw
Art by John Joffre
- AND LED ME TO THE BEST ILLUSTRATOR EVER!

To Catch a Cloud
by Bronchelle Parker
Art by Joanne Lew-Vriethoff

Monroe Pelly Can
By Bronchelle Parker
Art by Jennifer L. Meyer

The Gift
By Roderick J. Robinson
Art by Laura Montenegro

My Brother, Joshua
By Nola Hushing
Art by Michael Chesworth

Coconuts
By Dagmar Kost
Art by Jade Rowland

Taste's Good
By Kathleen Weidner Zoehfeld
Art by Thor Wickstrom

Career Cat
By Irene A. Flores
Art by Phoenix Chan
Library For All Ltd.

Poison or Medicine?
Are you poison or medicine?
Yes.

The Frog's Prints
By Margaret Mincks
Art by Paul Meisel

www.ingramcontent.com/pod-product-compliance
Lightning Source LLC
Chambersburg PA
CBHW040317050426
42452CB00018B/2885